MOM MOM AND ME

KAREN GAIL

Copyright © 2024

Karen Gail

ISBN

All reasonable attempts have been made to verify the accuracy of the information provided in this publication. Nevertheless, the author assumes no responsibility for any errors and/or omissions.

Contents

Mom Mom and Me!

Introduction

This book isn't just about fun times with my grandchildren. It's for all children, big and small. It's about having fun, being creative, building relationships, and spending time with those you love. Remember…everyday spent together leaves more memories.

Embrace those you love. Be sure to let them know how you feel. 

This book is for Grandmoms everywhere, no matter what nickname you use.

Dedicated to five super special people in my life:

Beckett, Kallie, Hailey, Dashiell, and Arden

Thank you for your inspiration.

I love you all to the moon and back!

Mom Mom loves to draw and also to paint.

Chapter 1: "A Fun Day with Mom Mom"

Once upon a sunny Saturday morning, the doorbell rang. It was Mom Mom's twin granddaughters, Kallie and Hailey! They always have the best time together. Their faces were beaming with excitement as they rushed in. "Hi, Mom Mom!" they both chimed, practically bursting with joy.

"Hello, my little adventurers! Are you ready for a day full of fun?" Mom Mom asked, grinning widely. The day started by setting up a huge art space. The table was covered in paints, crayons, markers, and was a blank canvas ready for exciting imaginations.

As they drew and painted, their minds went on amazing journeys. Hailey drew a rainbow unicorn, and Kallie made a galaxy filled with stars. Their artwork was so cool! "It's like magic, Mom Mom! Look, my unicorn is flying over the rainbow!" Hailey said, her eyes shining with excitement. "Kallie, your galaxy looks like it's hiding lots of secret stories among the stars," Mom Mom said, amazed by her creativity. The art wasn't just lines and colors; it was like a happy dance on paper, just like the fun in their hearts.

After their artsy adventure, it was time for some outdoor fun! They wore their roller skates, and off they went, wobbling a bit but having a blast. Kallie and Hailey held Mom Mom's hands as they glided down the sidewalk. They felt like they were skating in their very own magical world.

Sometimes she likes to roller skate.

"Mom Mom, look! I can skate backward!" Kallie said proudly, showing off her new skill. "And Hailey, your spins are amazing! You could be a roller skating pro soon," Mom Mom cheered, watching her twirl around happily. They giggled and laughed as they rolled around the neighborhood, making memories that felt super special. It wasn't just about skating; it was about the happy moments they shared.

As the day came to an end, they sat down with some yummy hot chocolate and cookies. The girls talked about the day, sharing stories and dreams. The love and happiness felt in those moments was so wonderful.

"My sweet grandkids, today has been magical. It's not just about what we did, but about how much fun we had, how close we felt, and the cool memories we made together," Mom Mom said, holding their hands. "Mom Mom, we love hanging out with you. You make everything so fun!" Kallie grinned.

"Yeah, it's like we have our own secret world when we're with you," Hailey added, giving Mom Mom a big hug. "Tomorrow will be even more fun when your cousins arrive." And in that moment, Mom Mom's heart felt so full. It wasn't just about being a Mom Mom; it was about being a friend, playing games, and making awesome memories together.

She likes to play games like hide and seek.

Sometimes we don't find her for over a week.

5

Chapter 2: "Adventures in the Neighborhood"

The next day, the grandchildren from many miles away arrived for a fun week with Mom Mom and their cousins. Beckett, Dash, and Arden arrived, all chanting, "Mom Mom!" with contagious excitement.

"Hello, my little people! Are you all set for a day filled with fun?" Mom Mom greeted them, her heart swelling with joy at the sight of the expanded team of explorers.

With all of the cousins together, they decided to embark on new adventures. After everyone settled in from their long drive, they decided to play some games. Hide and seek was the game everyone voted on, and Dash, with his quick moves, was an expert at finding secret hiding spots.

"Found you, Bex!" Dash gleefully exclaimed, revealing a hidden play area. Kallie was found curled up under a table, Hailey was in the pantry closet, and Arden was found under a chair.

As usual, Mom Mom was found behind the sofa…her favorite hiding spot. They all took turns being the finder, and it was so much fun.

Following the games, the expanded group mounted their bikes and put on their helmets, ready for a ride through the neighborhood. Bex, the trailblazer, led everyone down secret paths and through enchanting shortcuts, revealing hidden treasures along the way. They all marveled at the little ladybugs, butterflies, and beautiful trees and flowers they saw.

"Look, everyone! I found a secret passage through the enchanted woods," Bex announced proudly. It was a path through the neighborhood!

She likes to take bicycle rides down the street.

Every so often, she bakes a sweet treat.

As the day rolled on, their noses were greeted by a delightful aroma. It was the scent of the sweet treats that had been baked the day before – pumpkin pies, chocolate pudding and chocolate chip cookies. With each bite, their taste buds danced with joy, savoring the sweetness of their shared creations. Arden made everyone a glass of chocolate milk to go with their sweets. She is so good at it!

"Arden, you've got chocolate on your cheek!" giggled Hailey, pointing to her little cousin's face.

As the golden light of day began to fade, everyone settled in and they each shared their favorite adventures of the day. Everyone was tired and ready to sleep.

"Today was awesome, Mom Mom! I love hanging out with everyone," Hailey beamed.

"Yeah, it's like our very own secret world of fun and excitement," Kallie added, giving Mom Mom a big, warm hug.

Having all the grandchildren together is a dream come true. It's like hosting a "cousin camp" so that they can create lasting memories of family.

In that beautiful moment, Mom Mom's heart swelled with happiness, feeling as if it might burst. This day of exploring and outdoor activities taught the value of togetherness, and the magic of shared experiences.

She loves to garden and plant pretty flowers.

Chapter 3: "Mom Mom's Garden"

The next day brought a gentle breeze, and the gang decided to check out Mom Mom's garden. It is her little piece of paradise with all sorts of pretty flowers she loves tending to. As the grandkids gathered, their eyes widened at the sight of the thriving garden.

"Hey, little adventurers! Today, we're diving into the wonders of Mom Mom's garden," Mom Mom declared, feeling the excitement in the air.

They got their hands dirty with gardening gloves, and Mom Mom passed out small shovels. The garden was waiting for their touch. Hailey, with her eyes sparkling like morning dew, carefully planted vibrant marigolds. Kallie, letting her artistic side shine, arranged daisies in a pattern that was all her own.

"Your flowers are going to make Mom Mom's garden even more beautiful," Mom Mom praised, truly impressed by their dedication.

Bex took on the watering can duty, while Dash, full of energy, happily watered the plants. Even little Arden, the smallest but no less enthusiastic, placed pebbles around the newly planted flowers.

As the day unfolded, Mom Mom's garden transformed into a colorful masterpiece of assorted flowers. Hours passed with each grandchild taking turns mowing the lawn with her. All one could hear was the hum of the lawnmower mixed with laughter and the occasional fluttering of butterflies. They each designed their own garden stepping stones with plaster and sea glass and placed them in the garden.

Sometimes she mows her lawn for hours and hours.

"Look, Mom Mom! We mowed the whole lawn!" Kallie announced proudly.

"And we watered all the plants!" added Hailey, her face beaming with accomplishment.

In the soft afternoon sun, they gathered in the shade, surrounded by the beauty and greenery of the garden. Their hands were dirty, but their hearts were full of joy. They talked about the importance of responsibility and appreciating nature.

"Taking care of the garden teaches us responsibility, just like taking care of each other does," Mom Mom explained, the warmth of the moment sinking in.

The grandkids nodded, understanding that the vibrant blooms around them weren't just pretty flowers; they were a result of their shared dedication and care.

The lesson wasn't just about gardening; it was about nurturing, growing, and appreciating the beauty that comes from collective care.

Mom Mom hugged every grandchild, grateful for the day spent among the flowers and for the artistic touches they each added to the garden. "Hopefully, the weather will be nice for our day tomorrow!" she said.

She loves to sit on the beach and watch the waves roll in.

Chapter 4: "A Day at the Beach"

The sun climbed high, signaling a perfect day for the family's beach adventure. Armed with buckets, shovels, and towels, the group headed for the shore, ready for a day of sand and sea.

The grandkids' eyes lit up at the sight of the vast beach, and soon, it became a playground for sandcastles. Laughter filled the air as towers and bridges took shape. Hailey added seashell decorations, Kallie crafted intricate seaweed patterns, and the boys collaborated on an epic sand kingdom. Little Arden, in her own adorable way, contributed to the sandy masterpiece.

Proud of their creations, they strolled along the boardwalk, lured by the smell of saltwater taffy and the distant sounds of carnival music. Carnival games beckoned, and the grandkids eagerly tried their luck. Cheers erupted as rings landed on bottles, and prizes were claimed with beaming smiles.

Exploring the boardwalk, they indulged in cotton candy, captured moments with photos, and reveled in the lively atmosphere. Riding the Ferris wheel gave all of them the beautiful view of the shoreline, where the ocean and the sky meet. Dash and Bex were daring and took a glorious ride on the roller coaster. Then it was on to a competitive round of miniature golf.

Back on the sand, the grandkids partook in various beach activities – chasing waves, collecting seashells, and trying their hand at beach volleyball.

As the day waned, they gathered on beach blankets, the sun setting in the background. Seagulls called out overhead, bidding farewell to a day well spent.

Then she walks on the boardwalk to look for a prize she can win.

"Today was amazing, Mom Mom! I loved building sandcastles and winning prizes!" Hailey exclaimed.

"Yeah, and the beach games were so much fun!" added Kallie, her eyes sparkling.

"Mom Mom, can we do this again soon?" asked Dash, his eyes reflecting the genuine excitement of the day.

"Absolutely, my little adventurer. There are more beaches to explore and more fun things to do," Mom Mom replied, a twinkle in her eye.

As the sun dipped below the horizon, they packed up their belongings. A day at the beach not only filled their hearts with laughter but also brought them closer to each other.

The next day will bring more surprises.

She loves to shop and buy lots of things.

Sometimes she even tries to sing!

Chapter 5: "Mom Mom's Shopping Spree"

The weekend was here, bringing with it a special tradition – shopping with Mom Mom! It was like stepping into a dream come true, a day to find little treasures and have some fun.

Mom Mom entered the bustling mall with a glint in her eye, much like a kid entering a candy store. The grandkids, all excited for the upcoming adventure, exchanged knowing looks, ready for the day of exploration. With shopping bags in hand, they eagerly dove into the maze of shops, ready for whatever surprises awaited them.

Their first stop was Mom Mom's favorite department store. Hailey and Kallie, the inseparable duo, stuck close to Mom Mom, sharing smiles as she marveled at each item.

"Hailey, check this out! Isn't this shade of blue just beautiful?" Mom Mom exclaimed, holding up a flowy summer dress.

Kallie, just as captivated, nodded in agreement. "Absolutely! You'd look amazing in that, Mom Mom."

Bex, Dash, and Arden joined in the fun, offering their thoughts on what Mom Mom should buy. What started as a shopping trip quickly turned into a lively fashion show, with Kallie, Hailey, and Arden twirling in different dresses, much to their delight.

"Mom Mom, those sunglasses are a must! You look like a movie star!" Dash suggested...his laughter infectious. Mom Mom, always up for a good time, struck a pose.

The grandkids, each in their unique way, contributed to the spree. Bex helped choose items like challenging games and puzzles. Dash recommended Mom Mom try on sneakers for their bicycle rides and walks. Arden pointed out the vibrant colors that caught her fancy. Of course, each grandchild got to pick out something to take home that they would enjoy.

They then visited the mall's food court for a quick snack and the grandkids shared stories about their favorite finds and amusing moments.

"Today was a blast, Mom Mom! Who knew shopping could be this fun?" Hailey exclaimed, sipping on her smoothie.

"Yeah, and you're the coolest shopper ever!" Kallie added a mischievous twinkle in her eyes.

With smiles all around, Mom Mom's heart swelled with love.

Shop

She loves dogs, of which she's had many, and other animals too- Milton the cat, and those at the zoo…just to name a few.

Chapter 6: "Mom Mom and the Animals"

Mom Mom loves animals, especially dogs. Champ, Peanut, Rocky and Cody were, and are, all members of the family. Milton is a playful and mischievous cat who lives with Kallie and Hailey. He's a furry member of the family who has a way of making everyone smile.

A memorable trip to the zoo was a day full of wonder for the grandkids. Mom Mom's eyes shone with excitement as she shared fun facts about each animal they encountered. Bex loved the roar of the lions, while Dash was thrilled watching monkeys swing around. Hailey and Kallie were fascinated by the graceful giraffes, and little Arden's giggles were delightful as she watched the playful otters.

Then, there was a visit to a farm with goats, cows, pigs, and bunnies. All the children got to feed the goats and pigs with carrots and kale. It was so much fun.

But the real excitement was at home. Mom Mom's love for dogs turned their house into a cozy haven for furry pals. Each grandkid had a special bond with these pets, learning important lessons about love and caring. From playing in the yard to cozy cuddles indoors, these moments were filled with warmth and joy.

Their time with animals wasn't just about the zoo or their pets; it was about learning to be kind and understanding. Mom Mom believed that looking after animals taught important lessons about being gentle and responsible. Every pet, from the dogs to Milton the playful cat, taught the grandkids to care and be compassionate. Having pets also reminds us that they are animals first, and we must be careful not to interrupt their eating or sleeping.

As the grandkids grew, their love for animals grew too. They learned that animals, like people, needed love and care. Mom Mom's house wasn't just a place for the family; it was a safe space for animals, where everyone learned to care for and understand them better.

Through their experiences with animals, the grandkids learned that a little kindness goes a long way. They discovered that animals had feelings too and needed love and attention. Mom Mom's love for animals became a lasting lesson, showing them the wonderful bond between people and their furry friends.

Sometimes she likes to swing on the swings.

Chapter 7: "The Last Day"

As the week came to an end, they all reminisced about all the fun things they had done. They painted, drew and created. They roller-skated through the neighborhood. Riding bikes together was so much fun. They played hide and seek. They baked pies and cookies, and then they ate them.

They worked in the garden planting pretty flowers and mowed the lawn with a real riding mower.

They went to the beach where the grandkids built sandcastles, collected shells, and swam in the ocean. They walked on the boardwalk where fun prizes were won. They visited the zoo and the farm and took care of Cody and Milton, which was a lot of fun.

They gathered in the backyard, climbed on the play set, and swung on the swings. They had soooo much fun together.

They all played together one last time before the cousins had to leave to go home. They talked about all the new adventures of the week, and how much they had grown with each experience.

Waving goodbye to Beckett, Dashiell, and Arden was heartbreaking, but they will all see each other again soon. Then it will be time to do all the things they did this week and try some new fun things as well.

The grandkids give Mom Mom a purpose, a reason to still do all the things kids do, and they fill her heart more than they will ever know. Even though the week is over, Mom Mom is already planning for the next time all of the cousins will be together. She knows that if not for Beckett, Kallie, Hailey, Dashiell, and Arden, she wouldn't be Mom Mom. And it's only the beginning.

Mom Mom likes to do a lot of things, you see. But, she wouldn't be Mom Mom if it wasn't for me!

Dash   Kallie   Hailey   Arden   Bex